DREAMS CAN COME TRUE
- IT'S TIME TO BELIEVE IN YOU

BEDTIME STORY

ENGLISH ◆ FRENCH ◆ SPANISH ◆ GERMAN ◆
ITALIAN ◆ PORTUGUESE ◆ CHINESE

I0441327

NATASHA PARKER

Copyright © 2012 por Natasha Parker.

www.HarmonyHealthandHappiness.com
luisanatashaparker@hotmail.co.uk

ISBN: Tapa Blanda   978-1-4633-3432-1
                    Libro Electrónico   978-1-4633-4615-7

Todos los derechos reservados. Ninguna parte de este libro puede ser reproducida o transmitida de cualquier forma o por cualquier medio, electrónico o mecánico, incluyendo fotocopia, grabación, o por cualquier sistema de almacenamiento y recuperación, sin permiso escrito del propietario del copyright.

Illustrations by: Eumir Carlo Fernandez

Este Libro fue impreso en los Estados Unidos de América.

**Para pedidos de copias adicionales de este libro,
por favor contacte con:**
Palibrio
1663 Liberty Drive
Suite 200
Bloomington, IN 47403
Llamadas desde los EE.UU. 877.407.5847
Llamadas internacionales +1.812.671.9757
Fax: +1.812.355.1576
ventas@palibrio.com
[384093]

ESPECIALLY FOR

特別是對

SPECIALEMENT POUR VOUS

ESPECIALMENTE PARA

ESPECIALMENTE PARA

(Name)

ESPECIALE PER

SPEZIALL FUR

"Dreams es un interesante compendio de pequeñas, pero gigantes reflexiones que recopila Natasha Parker para sembrar en cada espíritu infantil la semilla que les permita crear huellas, trascender en lo espiritual y tener una brújula de valores que los oriente ante las vicisitudes del mundo material"

Mariana Orea
Directora Ejecutiva

GRUPO
EDITORIAL
LATITUD21

DREAMS CAN COME TRUE

RECOMENDATION/RECOMENDACIONES/EMPFEHLUNG/ SUI CONSIGLI /RECOMENDAÇÃO/速遞熱力推薦

I know that there are so many people in the World who come from different backgrounds and beliefs and under no circumstances do I want to impose or change them. For this reason, I recommend changing the word God for I or MUM or DAD, or any other special person or word you want to use.

Je sais qu'il ya tant de gens dans le monde qui viennent d'horizons différents et des croyances et en aucun cas ce que je veux imposer ou de les modifier. Pour cette raison, je vous recommandons de changer le mot Dieu pour maman ou papa, ou toute autre personne ou mot spéciale que vous souhaitez utiliser.

Se que existen tantas personas en el Mundo que vienen de diferentes antecedentes y sus creencias y en ningún circunstancia quiero imponer o cambiarlas. Por esta razón, recomendo que cambien la palabra Dios por YO o MAMA o PAPA, o cualquier otra persona o palabra especial que quieran usar.

Ich weiß, dass es so viele Menschen in der Welt, die aus verschiedenen Hintergründen und Überzeugungen kommen und unter keinen Umständen will ich zu verhängen oder zu ändern. Aus diesem Grund empfehle ich dem Ändern des Wortes Gottes für Ich oder Mama oder Papa, oder jede andere spezielle Person oder Wort, die Sie verwenden möchten.

So che ci sono così tante persone nel mondo, che provengono da esperienze diverse e credenze e in nessun caso voglio imporre o modificarli. Per questo motivo, vi consiglio di cambiare la parola Dio per I o mamma o papà, o di qualsiasi altra persona speciale o una parola che si desidera utilizzare.

Eu sei que há muitas pessoas no mundo que vêm de diferentes origens e crenças e sob nenhuma circunstância que eu quero impor ou alterá-las. Por esta razão, eu recomendo mudar a palavra Deus para que eu ou mãe ou pai, ou qualquer outra pessoa ou palavra especial que você quer usar.

我知道世界上有這麼多的人來自不同背景和信仰，並在任何情況下，我想他們施加或更改。出於這個原因，我建議改變神對我和媽媽或爸爸，或其他任何特殊的人或你想使用的字

Name/Nom/Nombre/Name/Nome/Nome/名稱:-

****

REMEMBER TODAY AND EVERY DAY ……

N'OUBLIEZ PAS AUJOURD'HUI ET CHAQUE JOUR …

RECUERDA HOY Y CADA DIA….

ERINNERN HEUTE UND JEDEN TAG ….

RICORDA OGGI E OGNI GIORNO …

LEMBRE-SE HOJE E TODOS OS DIAS ….

還記得今天和每一天

God Loves Your Enthusiasm For Life. Every Moment
Is A Chance To Make Your Dreams Come True.

Dieu aime votre enthousiasme pour la vie. Chaque moment
est une chance de faire vos rêves deviennent réalité.

Dios Te Quiere Por Tu Entusiasmo Por La Vida. Cada Momento
Es Una Oportunidad Para Hacer Tus Sueños Realidad.

Gott Liebt Ihre Begeisterung Für Leben. Jeder Moment
Ist Eine Möglichkeit, Ihre Träume Zu machen, erfüllte Sich.

Dio ama il tuo entusiasmo per la vita. Ogni momento
è la possibilità di fare i vostri sogni.

Deus Ama O Entusiasmo Pela Vida. Cada Momento
É Uma Oportunidade De Fazer Seus Sonhos Realidade.

神愛你對生活的熱情。每一刻都是一個機會，使你夢想成真

God Loves Your Understanding Of Others
And To Accept And Love Them For Who They Are.

Dieu Aime Votre Compréhension Des Autres
Et D'accepter Et De Aimer Pour Ce Qu'ils Sont.

Dios Te Quiere Por Tu Comprensión De Otros
Y De Aceptar Y Quererlos Por Quien Son.

Gott Liebt Euer Verständnis Für Andere
Und Zu Akzeptieren Und Zu Lieben, Wie Sie Sind.

Dio Ama La Tua Comprensione Degli Altri
E Di Accettare E Amarli Per Quello Che Sono.

Deus Ama A Sua Compreensão Dos Outros
E De Aceitar E Amá-Los Pelo Que São.

上帝愛你對他人的理解，接受和愛他們，他們是誰。

God Loves Your Thoughtfulness Towards Others
With Your Words, Your Thoughts, Your Actions.

Dieu Aime Votre Gentillesse Envers Les Autres
Avec Vos Mots, Vos Pensées, Vos Actions.

Dios Te Quiere Por Tu Amabilidad Hacia Otros
Con Tus Palabras, Tus Pensamientos Y Tus Acciones.

Gott Liebt Ihr Rücksichtnahme Gegenüber Anderen
Mit Ihren Worten, Eure Gedanken, Eure Aktionen.

Dio Ama La Tua Premura Verso Gli Altri Con Le Vostre Parole,
I Vostri Pensieri, Le Vostre Azioni.

Deus Ama O Seu Consideração Para Com Os Outros
Com Suas Palavras, Seus Pensamentos, Suas Ações.

上帝愛你的體貼你的話，你的思想，你的行動對他人

God Loves Your Persistence To Never Give Up, No Matter The Circumstances Or How Difficult The Task. You Can Do It.
Yes You Can.

Dieu Aime Votre Persistance A Ne Jamais Abandonner Peu Importe Les Circonstances Ou La Difficulté De La Tâche. Vous Pouvez Le Faire. Oui, Vous Pouvez.

Dios Te Quiere Por Tu Persistencia De Nunca Rendirte, No Importa Las Circunstancias O Que Difícil La Tarea. Tú Puedes Hacerlo.
Si Lo Puedes.

Dio Ama La Persistenza Di Non Mollare Mai Indipendentemente Dalle Circostanze O Come Difficile Il Compito. Puoi Farlo.
Sì, È Possibile.

Deus Ama A Sua Persistência Nunca Desistir Não Importa As Circunstâncias Ou Como Difícil Tarefa. Você Pode Fazer Isso.
Sim Você Pode.

上帝愛你的持久，永不放棄的情況下，無論多麼困難的任務。你可以做。是的，你可以

God Loves You for The Happiness And Joy You Bring To Others Around You With Your Laughter, Your Smile and Your Hugs.

Dieu Aime Le Bonheur Et La Joie Vous Apporter Aux Autres Autour De Vous Avec Votre Rire, Votre Sourire et Votre Embrasse.

Dios Te Quiere Por Tu Felicidad Y Alegría Que Entregas A Otros Con Tu Risa, Con Tu Sonrisa Y Tus Abrazos.

Gott Liebt Die Glück Und Freude Mitbringen, Um Andere Um Dich Herum Mit Dein Lachen, Dein Lächeln und Deinen Umarmungen.

Dio Ama La Felicità E La Gioia Che Portare Agli Altri Che Ti Circonda Con La Tua Risata, Il Tuo Sorriso I Vostri Abbracci.

Deus Ama A Felicidade E Alegria Que Você Traz Para Outros Ao Seu Redor Com Sua Risada, Seu Sorriso e Seu Abraços.

上帝愛你帶給你周圍的人的幸福和快樂，你的笑聲，你的微笑，你的擁抱

God Loves You For Your Intelligence, Hard Work And Dedication.
In Everything You Do.

Dieu Vous Aime Pour Votre Intelligence, Le Travail Acharné Et Le
Dévouement Avec Tous Que Vous Faites.

Dios Te Quiere Por Tu Inteligencia, Esfuerzo Y Dedicación En Todo
Lo Que Haces.

Gott Liebt Dich Für Ihre Intelligenz, Harte Arbeit Und Hingabe In
Alles Was Sie Tun.

Dio Ti Ama Per La Tua Intelligenza, Duro Lavoro E Dedizione In
Qualsiasi Cosa Facciate.

Deus Ama A Sua Inteligência, Trabalho Duro E Dedicação Em
Tudo Que Você Faz.

上帝愛你，你的智慧，辛勤工作和奉獻精神做任何事都

God Loves You For The Love You Have Deep In Your Heart And Which You Share With Everyone With Your Kind Words.

Dieu Vous Aime Pour L'amour Vous Avez
En Profondeur Dans Votre Coeur Et Que Vous Partager
Avec Tout Le Monde Avec Votre Aimable Paroles.

Dios Te Quiere Por El Amor Que Tienes Dentro De Tu Corazón
Y Que Compartes Con Todos Con Tus Amables Palabras.

Gott Liebt Dich Für Die Liebe Sie Haben Tief In Deinem Herzen
Und Die Sie Mit Jedem Teilen Mit Ihrer Art Worten.

Dio Ti Ama Per L'amore Che Hai Nel Profondo Del Tuo Cuore,
E Che Si Condivide Con Tutti Con Le Sue Gentili Parole.

Deus Ama Você Para O Amor Que Você Tem No Fundo Do Seu
Coração E Que Você Compartilha Com Todos Com Suas Amáveis
Palavras.

上帝愛你，你的愛在你的心裡有很深的，哪些是你和大家一起分享
你的客氣話

God Loves You For Strength And Courage To Stamp On Your Fears And Leave Them Behind. I Am Here To Listen.

Dieu Vous Aime De Résistance Et De Courage Au Timbre Sur Vos Peurs Et Les Laisser Derrière. Je Suis Ici Pour Ecouter.

Dios Te Quiere Por Tu Fuerza Y Valor De Pisotear A Tus Miedos Y Dejarlos Atrás. Estoy Aquí Para Escucharte.

Gott Liebt Dich Für Stärke Und Mut, Sich Auf Ihre Ängste Stempel Und Zurückgelassen Werden. Ich Bin Hier, Um Zuzuhören.

Dio Ti Ama Per Forza E Coraggio Di Timbro Su Le Tue Paure E Lasciarli. Io Sono Qui Per Ascoltare.

Deus Ama A Força Ea Coragem Para Carimbo Em Seus Medos E Deixá-Los. Eu Estou Aqui Para Ouvir.

上帝愛你的力量和勇氣，郵票上你的恐懼，把它們留。我在這裡聽

God Loves You For Your Knowledge To Do The Right Thing At Every Moment. I Am Beside You To Guide And Help You Along The Way.

Dieu Vous Aime Pour Vos Connaissances À Faire Ce Qui Est Juste A Chaque Instant. Je Suis Près De Vous Pour Vous Guider Et Vous Aider A Su Le Chemin.

Dios Te Quiere Por Tu Conocimiento De Hacer Lo Correcto A Cada Momento. Estoy Contigo Para Guiarte Y Ayudarte En Tu Camino.

Gott Liebt Dich Für Ihr Wissen Zu Tun, Was Jedem Moment Zu Korrigieren. Ich Bin Neben Dir Zu Führen Und Zu Helfen Ihnen Auf Dem Weg.

Dio Ti Ama Per La Vostra Conoscenza Di Fare Ciò Che È Corretto In Ogni Momento. Sono Accanto A Voi Per Guidarvi E Aiutarvi Nel Vostro Cammino.

Deus Ama A Sua Conhecimento Para Fazer O Que É Correto A Cada Momento. Eu Sou Seu Lado Para Orientar E Ajudá-Lo Em Seu Caminho.

上帝愛你，你的知識，做正確的事，在每一個時刻。
我是在你身邊，引導和幫助你前進的道路

God Loves You Because You Live Every Moment Today And Leave The Past Behind. To Open The Door To Your Dreams Of The Future.

Dieu Vous Aime Parce Que Vous Vivre Chaque Instant Aujourd'hui Et Laisser Le Passé Derrière. Pour Ouvrir La Porte De Vos Rêves De Le Futur.

Dios Te Quiere Porque Vives Cada Instante Hoy Y Dejas El Pasado Atrás Para Abrir La Puerta A Tu Sueños Del Futuro.

Gott Liebt Dich, Weil Du Jeden Moment Leben Heute Und Lassen Sie Die Vergangenheit Hinter Sich. Die Tür Zu Ihren Traum Von Der Zukunft Zu Öffnen.

Dio Ti Ama Perche 'Oggi Vivere Ogni Momento E Lasciare Il Passato Alle Spalle. Per Aprire La Porta Ai Tuoi Sogni Del Futuro.

Deus Ama Você Porque Você Vive Cada Momento De Hoje E Deixar O Passado Para Trás. Para Abrir A Porta A Seus Sonhos Do Futuro.

上帝愛你是因為你生活的每一刻今天將過去拋在腦後。
打開大門，你對未來的憧憬。

You Are The Most Wonderful Person In The Whole World.

Vous Etes La Personne La Plus Merveilleuse Dans Le Monde Entier.

Tu Eres la Persona Mas Maravilloso En Todo El Mundo.

Sie Sind Die Schönsten Personen In Der Ganzen Welt.

Tu Sei La Persona Più Bella In Tutto Il Mondo.

Você É A Pessoa Mais Maravilhosa Do Mundo Inteiro.

你是最美妙的人，整個世界

God Loves You For Creativity, When You Paint,
You Sing, You Dance And Play.

Dieu Vous Aime Pour La Créativité, Lorsque Vous Peignez,
Vous Chantez, Vous Dansez Et Jouez.

Dios Te Quiere Por Tu Creatividad, Cuando Pintas,
Bailas, Y Juegas.

Gott Liebt Dich Für Ihre Kreativität, Wen Sie Malen,
Singen Sie, Tanzen Sie Und Sie Spielen.

Dio Ti Ama Per La Tua Creatività, Quando Si Dipinge,
Si Canta, Si Balla E Si Gioca.

Deus Ama Você Para Sua Criatividade, Quando Você Pinta,
Você Canta, Você Dançar E Jogar.

上帝愛你，你的創造力，當你畫的，你唱歌，你跳舞的和你玩

God Doesn´t Care How You Look, You Are Special Always,
Your Hair, Your Face, Your Body And Your Smile.

Dieu Ne S'inquiète Pas Votre Apparence, Vous Etes Spécial,
Vos Cheveux, Votre Visage, Votre Corps Et Votre Sourire.

Dios No Importa Cómo te Mires, Eres Especial,
Tu Cabello, Tu Cara, Tu Cuerpo, Y Tu Sonrisa.

Gott Ist Es Egal, Wie Du Aussiehst, Sind Sie Special,
Deine Haare, Dein Gesicht, Deine Körper Und Ihre Lächeln.

Dio Non Si Cura Come Si Guarda, Tu Sei Speciale,
I Tuoi Capelli, Il Tuo Volto, Il Tuo Corpo E Il Tuo Sorriso.

Deus Não Se Importa Como Você Olha, Você É Especial,
Seu Cabelo, Seu Rosto, Seu Corpo, E Seu Sorriso.

上帝不關心你怎麼看，你是特別的，你的頭髮，你的臉，
你的身體，你的微笑

God Loves You Exactly The Way You Are, Don´t Ever Change.

Dieu Vous Aime Exactement Ce Que Vous Etes, Ne Changera Jamais.

Dios Te Quiere Exactamente Como Eres, No Quiero Que Te Cambies.

Gott Liebt Dich Genau So Wie Du Bist, Nicht Immer Ändern.

Dio Ti Ama Esattamente Come Sei, Non Cambiare Mai.

Deus Ama Você Exatamente Como Você É, Não Mudar Nunca.

上帝愛你到底你的方式，永遠不要

God Wants You To Be Healthy
And Happy Enjoying Every Day.

Dieu Veut Que Vous Soyez Heureux Et En Santé
Et Profiter De Chaque Jour.

Dios Solo Quiere Que Estés Sano Y Feliz
Y Disfrutando De Cada Día.

Gott Möchte, Dass Gesund Und Glücklich Sein
Und Jeden Tag Genießen.

Dio Vuole Che Tu Essere Sani E Felici
E Godere Ogni Giorno.

Deus Quer Que Você Ser Saudável E Feliz
E Desfrutar Todos Os Dias.

上帝要你健康快樂，享受每一天

God Loves You When You Are At School, At Home,
Eating And Sleeping And Every Day.

Dieu Vous Aime Quand Vous Êtes À L'école, À La Maison,
Youâ Mangez Et Vous Dormez Chaque Jour.

Dios Te Quiere Cuando Estas En La Escuela, En Casa,
Comiendo Y Durmiendo Cada Día.

Gott Liebt Dich, Wenn Sie In Der Schule, Zu Hause Sind,
Sie Essen Und Du Schläfst Jeden Tag.

Dio Ti Ama Quando Sei In Scuola, A Casa,
Si Sta Mangiando E Si Dorme Ogni Giorno.

Deus Te Ama Quando Você Está Na Escola, Em Casa,
Você Está Comendo E Você Está Dormindo Todos Os Dias.

上帝愛你的時候你是在學校，在家裡，你在吃東西，你是每天睡覺

God Is Always With You To Listen To You And Will Be By Your Side Day And Night - No Matter Where You Are Or How Old You Are.

Dieu Est Toujours Avec Vous Pour Ecouter Vous Et Sera Par Votre Côté Jour Et Nuit - Peu Importe Où Vous Etes Ou Comment Vieux Vous Etes.

Dios Esta Siempre Contigo Para Escucharte Y Siempre Estará A Tu Lado Día Y Noche - No Importa Donde Estés O Cuantos Años Tienes.

Gott Ist Immer Mit Ihnen Um Ihnen Zuzuhören Und An Ihrer Seite Werden Tag Und Nacht - Egal, Wo Sie Sind Oder Wie Alt Du Bist.

Dio E ,Sempre Con Te Per Ascoltare Voi E Sara' Al Tuo Fianco Giorno E Notte - Non Importa Dove Sei O Quanti Anni Hai.

Deus Está Sempre Com Você Ouvir Você E Vai Estar Ao Seu Lado Dia E Noite - Não Importa Onde Você Está Ou Quantos Anos Você Tem.

神總是與你聽你的，並會在你身邊的晝夜 - 無論你在哪裡，你怎麼老

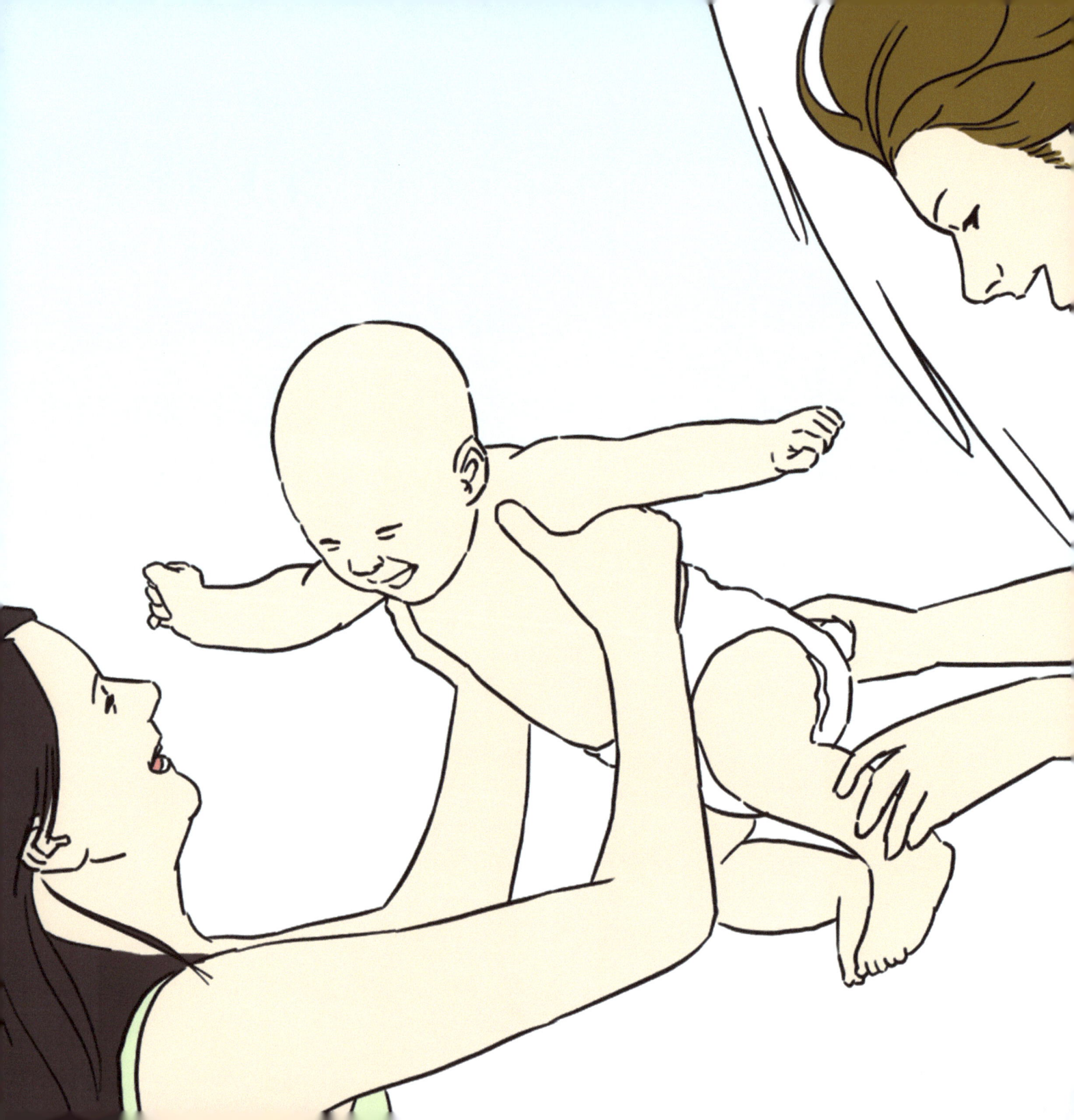

Today And Always You Are A Wonderful Child And
That's Why God Loves You For Ever And Ever.

Aujourd'hui Et Toujours Vous Êtes Un Enfant Merveilleux
Et C'est Pourquoi Dieu Vous Aime Eternellement.

Hoy Y Siempre Tu Eres Un Maravilloso Niño/Niña
Y Por Eso Dios Te Quiere Eternamente.

Heute Und Immer Sie Sind Ein Wunderbares Kind,
Und Deshalb Gott Liebt Dich Ewig.

Oggi E Sempre Sei Un Figlio Meraviglioso
E Ecco Perché Dio Ti Ama Eternamente.

Hoje E Sempre Você É Um Filho Maravilhoso
E É Por Isso Que Deus Te Ama Eternamente.

今天和永遠自己是一個很好的孩子，這就是為什麼上帝愛你，永遠

Our Father, Who is in heaven,
Holy is Your Name;
Your kingdom come,
Your will be done,
on earth as it is in heaven.Give
us this day our daily bread,
and forgive us our sins,
as we forgive those who sin
against us; and lead us not into
temptation,
but deliver us from evil. Amen.

Notre Père qui es aux cieux,
que ton Nom soit sanctifié,
que ton règne vienne,
que ta volonté soit faite
sur la terre comme au ciel.
Donne-nous aujourd'hui notre
pain de ce jour.Pardonne-nous
nos offenses,comme nous
pardonnons aussi à ceux qui
nous ont offensés.
Et ne nous soumets pas à la
tentation,mais délivre-nous du
mal.Amen

Padre nuestro,
que estás en el cielo,
santificado sea tu Nombre;
venga a nosotros tu reino;
hágase tu voluntad
en la tierra como en el cielo. Danos
hoy nuestro pan de cada día;
perdona nuestras ofensas,
como también nosotros
perdonamos a los que nos
ofenden;
no nos dejes caer en la tentación,
y líbranos del mal. Amén

Unser Vater im Himmel,
dein Name werde geheiligt,
dein Reich komme,
dein Wille geschehe
wie im Himmel, so auf der Erde.
Gib uns heute das Brot, das
wir brauchen. Und erlaß uns
unsere Schulden, wie auch
wir sie unseren Schuldnern
erlassen haben.
Und führe uns nicht in
Versuchung,
sondern rette uns vor dem
Bösen. Amen

Pater noster, qui es in caelis;
sanctificetur nomen tuum;
adveniat regnum tuum;
fiat voluntas tua,
sicut in caelo et in terra.
Panem nostrum cotidianum da
nobis hodie;
et dimitte nobis debita nostra,
sicut et nos dimittimus
debitoribus nostris;et ne nos
inducas in tentationem;sed
libera nos a malo Amen

Pai nosso, que estás no céu,
Santificado seja o Vosso nome.
Venha a nós o Vosso reino.
Seja feita a Vossa vontade,
Assim na terra como no céu.
O pão nosso de cada dia nos dai
hoje.Perdoai as nossas ofensas
Assim como nós perdoamos a
quem nos têm ofendido.Não nos
deixeis cair em tentação,Mas livrai-
nos do mal. Amen

我們在天上的父,
願人都尊祢的名為聖,
願祢的國降臨,
願祢的旨意行在地上,
如同行在天上。
我們日用的飲食,
今日賜給我們,
免我們的債,
如同我們免了人的債,
不叫我們遇見試探,
救我們脫離兇惡,
因為國度、權柄、榮耀,全是祢的,
直到永遠。阿們!

May Your Dreams Come True And Be Filled With Happiness
And Love And Tomorrow You Awake With Health,
Love, Joy And Success In Everything You Do.

Que Vos Rêves Deviennent Réalité Et Etre Rempli De Bonheur
Et D'amour Et Demain Vous Avec Tout Éveillé Santé,
Amour, Joie Et Succès Que Vous Faire.

Que Tus Sueños Se Hagan Realidad Y Que Estén Llenos
De Felicidad Y Amor, Y Mañana Despiertas Con La Salud,
Amor, Alegría Y Éxito En Todo Lo Que Hagas.

Mögen Deine Träume Wahr Werden Und Mit Glück
Und Liebe Und Morgen Auszufüllen Sie Wachen Mit Gesundheit,
Liebe, Freude Und Erfolg In Allem Was Du Tust.

Maggio I Tuoi Sogni E Sia Colmo Di Felicità E
Di Amore E Domani Ti Svegli Con Salute, Amore,
Gioia E Successo In Qualsiasi Cosa Facciate.

Que Seus Sonhos E Ser Preenchido Com Felicidade
E Amor E Amanhã Você Acordar Com Saúde,
Amor, Alegria E Exito Em Tudo Que Faz.

願你的夢想成真，充滿了幸福和愛，明天你醒了與健康，
愛，喜悅和成功，你所做的一切

I LOVE YOU, I LOVE YOU, I LOVE YOU

JE T'AIME, JE T'AIME, JE T'AIME

TE AMO, TE AMO, TE AMO

ICH LIEBE DICH, ICH LIEBE DICH,
ICH LIEBE DICH

TI AMO, TI AMO, TI AMO

EU TE AMO, EU TE AMO, EU TE AMO

我愛你，我愛你，我愛你

THANK YOU/MERCI/GRACIAS/DANKE/ GRAZIE/ OBRIGADO/謝謝！

EVERYONE/TOUT LE MONDE/TODOS/ALLE/TUTTI/大家

THE AUTHOR

Natasha Parker is a mother of three wonderful children. She has travelled and lived in many countries around the World. Originally from the UK and now living in Mexico.

She has worked in many industries throughout her career and studied many different alternative medicine therapies. At present she is a Sanacion Pranic therapist conducting crystal, psychotherapy, distant energy healing, bioplasma facial rejuvenation and energetic body sculpturing, to help people and children with their illnesses, emotions and pains in all aspects of their lives and to bring back the happiness and smiles to everyone where every they may be.

Luisa Natasha asks her readers to contact her - she would love to hear how your wonderful children are growing into the great people of tomorrow. Luisanatashaparker@hotmail.co.uk or visit www.HarmonyHealthandHappiness.com

www.ingramcontent.com/pod-product-compliance
Lightning Source LLC
Chambersburg PA
CBHW041512280526
45792CB00004B/1222